Anger Management
Activities for Kids

Anger Management
Activities for Kids

50+ Exercises for Understanding Feelings, Staying Calm, and Managing Strong Emotions

Holly Forman-Patel, MA, LMFT, LPCC

Illustrations by Claudio Cerri

ROCKRIDGE
PRESS

Interior and Cover Designer: Suzanne LaGasa
Art Producer: Sara Feinstein
Editor: Sam Barbaro
Production Editor: Jenna Dutton

Illustrations © 2020 Claudio Cerri

ISBN: Print 978-1-64611-629-4 | eBook 978-1-64611-630-0

R0

To all the kiddos I've worked with, past/present/ future, who felt that the anger monster was more powerful than them. You indeed are more powerful.

Contents

A Letter to Grown-Ups

Thank you for making the choice to pick up this book. I am guessing you are a caring adult in the life of a child who is having trouble with anger. You may be a teacher, parent, guardian, or therapist. Whatever your role is, the simple act of paying more attention to the emotional world of the child/children in your life is the first step in helping them gain the skills to conquer the anger monster.

Children express anger in a variety of ways: tantrums, hurtful words, acts of aggression, self-defeating comments, sadness, and so on. Anger is very common, especially in kids. Their entire world is being controlled for them, and often the only way they feel they have some control is through their anger. It is normal for young kids to express frustration, anxiety, and sadness through angry outbursts. It is by far the quickest way for them to let others know they are not happy with what is happening. Imagine a four-year-old in a kitchen with a parent. The parent is on the phone while making breakfast and doesn't hear the four-year-old asking for something. However, seeing a cup flying off the table will definitely get the parent's attention.

Behind any big behavioral/emotional expression, there is always a need that is not being met. As the grown-up, you are responsible for investigating the need and then helping the child resolve the need in a positive way.

There is a fine line between regular run-of-the-mill anger and something bigger, such as a response to a trauma, a developmental disorder (such as autism), or some other underlying issue. Regardless of what is behind the anger, this book will provide support. However, if any of these issues is greatly impacting a child, individual or family therapy might be a helpful adjunct.

This workbook has more than 50 kid-relatable, fun activities pulled from evidence-based therapies, including cognitive behavioral therapy, mindfulness, Eye Movement Desensitization and Reprocess Therapy (EMDR), and play therapy. The activities are designed to help younger kids understand that their anger is *not* bad and they can begin to do things that will help them control their anger instead of letting it control them.

Your ability to model the skills and consistently coach and support the child in your life will be a key factor in helping the child make positive and sustainable shifts around their anger. I hope that you will engage in each activity yourself as a way to join your child in making these changes.

Finally, research into child development has shown that anger and aggression are very common, especially in the first few years of life. This is partly due to younger children having less inhibition and poor self-regulation, along with a variety of other factors (e.g., environment, parenting, temperament). However, as children grow older, continued levels of aggression can be associated with social-adjustment challenges or, in some cases, mental health symptoms.

It's important to support young children in their efforts to manage their anger sooner rather than later. There are many effective ways to help children manage their anger, and my hope is that this book will guide you through the beginning steps.

A Letter to Kids: Everyone Gets the Angries

There is something REALLY important you need to know. Are you ready? It's okay to be angry. That's right. Anger is absolutely okay! Everyone gets angry, and it's completely normal.

But . . . things get tricky when we are getting in trouble because of our anger. We might also be hurting others or ourselves with our body or words.

Another thing you need to know is that YOU are more powerful than your anger. Maybe that's hard for you to believe. Sometimes it probably feels like your anger is controlling YOU and it seems to come out of nowhere. In this book, we will call it the anger monster—but if there is another name you want to call it, call it that!

There are many things that can make a person angry. What makes you angry might not make your friends or your siblings angry, or your parents angry. Sometimes anger is like a Halloween costume. Under the costume is something very different. In the same way, underneath your anger there might be something else going on. You might act like you are angry, but maybe you are really just hungry, tired, or sad.

This book will help you become an anger detective. You will learn the clues that tell you when anger is in your body. You will figure out where your anger is coming from and how to get it out in ways that are safe. You will get to know how your anger affects the people around you. And you will discover activities to do BEFORE the anger monster takes over. These activities will help YOU take control!

The activities in this book will teach you about anger, but they are also meant to be fun. Use your imagination as you try new ways to control your anger. Be creative!

Now go ahead and take a peek at the first activity. Then give it a try!

Chapter 1

Why Do I Get the Angries?

Bailey at the Bakery

Bailey is at a bakery with her aunt. They are waiting in line for her favorite breakfast food—a cinnamon bun. Yum! Someone cuts in line in front of them. When Bailey and her aunt get to the counter, they are told that the last cinnamon bun was just sold. There are only cranberry oat muffins left. Bleh!

This is SO unfair, Bailey thinks to herself. She stares at the person who cut in line, eyeing the cinnamon bun that they have in their hand. She feels even worse as she watches the cinnamon bun thief smile and take a big bite. Isn't it enough that they took what should have been hers? Now they have to rub it in?

Bailey kicks the trash can next to her. Her aunt looks at her and frowns. Then her aunt says, "Why do you have to get angry all the time? This is a treat. If you can't be nice, we are going to go."

Oh, great, now I'm in trouble! Bailey feels anger take over her body. She kicks the trash can again. She feels like she can't stop herself. At that point, her aunt has had enough and takes her home.

Bailey didn't get her cinnamon bun—or any treat at all. And she was sure a lecture from her parents would be coming next.

Has something like this ever happened to you? In life, many things happen that feel unfair. These things can then make us feel many different feelings, including anger. But if we can change the way we think about something that happens to us, it will actually change how we feel!

Bailey was doing what we call *extreme thinking*. Extreme thinking happens when we think there are only two choices, such as "it's fair" or "it's unfair." But if we think about a situation in a different way or add more choices or thoughts, it can change how we feel.

For example, after her outburst, Bailey could have thought to herself, *It's okay. People make mistakes and I made a mistake.* She could have told her aunt how she was feeling and asked if they could go to another bakery.

This chapter is about discovering and exploring the things that make us angry. Sometimes, it's not really what happened that is making us mad. It could be something that happened earlier in the day. It could even be because we are hungry or we didn't get enough sleep. It's easier to get angry when we don't take care of ourselves.

The activities in this chapter will help you begin to investigate your anger. Are you ready to become an anger detective?

Where Does Anger Come From?

Everyone gets angry sometimes, and that's totally okay. But what is anger? Anger is one of the many feelings, or emotions, that we feel in our brain and our body. Anger helps protect us. But when we are young and learning to control it, anger can be very tricky. When we are first learning to work on our anger, it can feel like the anger monster goes from sleeping to doing flips on a trampoline in less than two seconds!

Has your anger ever gotten really big, really fast, so that you felt like you had no control? Sometimes it can feel like anger is coming from nowhere. But something almost always has to happen first for it to come.

The list below describes ordinary things that might wake up the anger monster. For this activity, start by standing. For each thing that has woken your anger monster, clap your hands or jump up and down.

Someone took your toy.

A grown-up told you no.

A friend or brother or sister was mean to you.

You didn't get to do something you wanted to do.

You didn't get something you thought you would get.

You felt left out.

No one listened to you.

Something wasn't fair.

You felt like other people didn't understand you.

Good job! What did you learn? Did you discover anything that surprised you?

The Many Secret Identities of Anger

People often say, "I'm not angry!" Anger is a tricky feeling, and there are many words we use to describe anger. Below is a list of some of those words. For each word on the list, tell about a time that you felt that way. It could be something that happened in the past few days or a long time ago.

> Angry, mad
>
> Frustrated
>
> Grumpy, grouchy
>
> Furious
>
> Annoyed, irritated

You can think about anger as something that grows from something small to something really big. Here is one way to order the words in the list to show how anger grows.

1. Grumpy, grouchy
2. Annoyed, irritated
3. Frustrated
4. Angry, mad
5. Furious

When we start feeling frustrated (#3 on the anger meter), that's usually when the anger monster comes out.

The order of anger words might be a little different for different people. Below, fill in the spaces with your word order. Write the smallest anger feeling on the left side, with anger growing until you get to the biggest anger feeling, which is furious, on the right side. If you know another word for anger that's not on the list that you like better, go ahead and add it.

It's important to learn the order of your anger feelings, which we are going to call your *anger meter*. There are some activities we can do when the anger monster takes over and other activities we can do *before* it takes over. We will learn how to use the anger meter in other chapters.

Hot Buttons

In the first activity, you learned about different things that can wake up the anger monster. Now let's find out what your hot buttons are.

What's a hot button, you ask? Good question! Hot buttons are events, people, or things that begin to wake up the anger monster. We all have hot buttons. Sometimes we have the same hot buttons, but often the buttons are different.

We looked at nine hot buttons in the first activity. As a reminder, here they are again:

> Someone took your toy.
>
> A grown-up told you no.
>
> A friend or brother or sister was mean to you.
>
> You didn't get to do something you wanted to do.
>
> You didn't get something you thought you would get.
>
> You felt left out.
>
> No one listened to you.
>
> Something wasn't fair.
>
> You felt like other people didn't understand you.

Now answer the following questions for each of the hot buttons. If a hot button doesn't make you angry, then skip it. Once you have gone through the list, you will discover what your top three hot buttons are.

> When was the last time it happened?
>
> Does it happen every day? Just a few times a week? Only once in a while?
>
> Do you get in trouble for this?

Hot Buttons, Continued . . .

On the lines below, write down your top three hot buttons. These are the buttons that get you into the most trouble or are the hardest ones for you.

1. _____

2. _____

3. _____

Knowing what your hot buttons are will help you in two ways. First, it will help the grown-up doing this workbook with you learn what you struggle with the most so they can try to help you with it. Second, when you know what bothers you the most, you can begin to make friends with the anger monster.

Discovering more about anger and learning ways to deal with it is the main job of an anger detective. Great job taking the first steps to becoming a fantastic anger detective!

Hidden Stories

Did you know that we often tell ourselves very simple stories? Sometimes the stories are just one sentence long. We often don't even know we are doing this! These stories are like clues that can help us find out why the anger monster gets angry. The stories are often icky, negative, and not very helpful.

Later on in this workbook, you will learn how to use these stories to change the anger monster into your friend instead of your enemy.

For now, think about the story you heard earlier about Bailey at the bakery. What simple stories do you remember her telling herself? Ask the grown-up going through this workbook with you to reread the story to help.

Were you able to find a simple story? Here are two you might have found:

- My cinnamon bun was stolen, and it's SO unfair.
- There is NOTHING I can do to control my anger.

Now share with the grown-up reading this to you the last time you got really angry. What was the story you told yourself?

Next, look at your three hot buttons. Use a puppet (or a stuffed animal) and have it share a story about what was happening the last time your hot buttons were pushed. Do this for all three buttons so that you can practice being a detective and finding the simple stories. If it is too hard to find the stories yourself, ask the grown-up to help you.

Once you know the unhelpful stories you tell yourself, you can begin to change them into happier, more helpful stories.

Thought Battle

Great job figuring out some of the stories or thoughts that are not helpful in your life! Now that you know the stories and thoughts, what are you going to do with them? Well, battle them, of course! The best way to deal with an icky thought is to discover stronger and more helpful thoughts or stories that can battle the icky thought.

Remember the story about Bailey and the cinnamon bun? Bailey's extreme thoughts were also icky thoughts. They were stories that were not helpful.

Often, icky thoughts feed our anger. Anger loves icky thoughts because they make it grow bigger and stronger. So we need to make sure we don't feed the anger monster! We can do that by trying to remember happy thoughts or stories that can battle the icky thoughts.

For example, what if one of your thoughts is "No one loves me"? Well, you have to find a thought that proves the opposite. Can you think of two different thoughts that could battle the thought "No one loves me"?

Here are some ideas:

> I love me.
>
> My parents love me.
>
> My friends love me.
>
> My pet loves me.
>
> My brother/sister loves me.

Here's another example. Suppose you have the thought "It's so unfair!" Can you think of two stronger and more helpful thoughts? Here are a few ideas:

> Sometimes rules change, and it's okay.
>
> Sometimes things are fair, and sometimes they are unfair.
>
> I can talk with a grown-up if something is really unfair, and they will try to help me.
>
> I will get my turn soon.

Your mission is to become an expert at battling thoughts. Do you accept the challenge? When you notice an icky thought creeping into your head, battle it with stronger and more helpful thoughts.

Happy Thinking

It may sound simple, but the more we can think happy thoughts, the more we will feel better about ourselves. And the more we feel better about ourselves, the less we will feed the anger monster.

Let's practice noticing how our body feels when we say extreme or icky thoughts to ourselves instead of happy ones.

For this activity, stand up and say the following three statements in a row. Say them out loud! Pretend that you really mean them or feel them.

It's SO unfair!

I NEVER get anything I want!

No one listens to me EVER!

How are you feeling in your body? You might be feeling your heart beating fast. You might feel hotness in your face or hands or tummy. Maybe you even feel some anger or sadness.

Now say these three positive or happy thoughts out loud. Again, say them like you really mean them!

There are many times when things ARE fair.

It's OKAY if I don't get what I want. I can figure out something else, and it might actually be MORE FUN.

There are MANY people who LOVE and LISTEN to me.

When we think in a positive way and we change the unhelpful thoughts or stories we tell ourselves, we begin to feel less angry when our hot buttons are pushed.

Meet the Anger Monster

Anger can feel like a battle going on inside of us. The problem is that a battle usually has a winner and a loser.

Instead of seeing anger as an enemy we are trying to fight, try to remember that anger is on our team. It really is! Try picturing this in your head. Can you see yourself and anger wearing the same team sweater?

For this activity, get a piece of paper and some crayons, markers, or pencils—whatever you like to draw with. Draw a picture of what you think your anger monster looks like. Does it look like a person or an animal? Does it look like a blob, or maybe an alien? Think about what its face and body look like. Try to add as many details as you can.

When you are done, you can even give your anger monster a name!

The Anger Volcano

It's really important for us to listen to our anger monster. If we don't listen to what it is saying, the monster is probably going to get louder and louder. It wants to get our attention. It might even start screaming at us!

When this happens, we might feel like we are losing control or like our anger came out of nowhere. This is usually when we do something that we are not proud of. We might scream, say mean things, or even use our hands and body to hurt someone or something.

The next two activities will give you an idea of what happens when we let our anger build up. You might want to wear old clothes or a painting apron. And you might want to do the activities outside!

Soda Explosion

Get a can of soda, but don't open it yet. Now think of five things that made you angry this week. Every time you think of something, shake the can up and down. Shake it just once, but very hard.

After you remember five things and shake the can five times, open the can. You can ask a grown-up to help you with this. What happened when you opened the can? Soda sprayed all over everything, right?

Anger is like the soda in the can, especially when we are first learning to work on it. If one of our hot buttons is pushed one or two times, there's a big anger explosion!

Remember our anger meter? (See the second activity in this chapter, "The Many Secret Identities of Anger," page 5.) The exploding soda shows how fast our anger can go from 0 to 5. Anger explosions can easily happen when someone is just beginning to work on their anger. There will be fewer explosions once you are able to control the anger monster.

Water Bomb

You can do this activity with a real balloon, or you can just use your imagination and pretend to do it.

Get a balloon, or imagine one. Now fill it up with water. As you watch the balloon get larger and larger, think of anger building up. Let the balloon get really big.

What happened? Did the balloon pop, or did water start spilling out? Things got kind of wet and messy, didn't they?

This is what happens to our anger if we let it build up and don't do anything. If our anger reaches 3 on the meter, something is about to happen. Once it goes to 5, it's really hard to control. But if you learn to notice your anger as it's growing, you can stop it before it explodes. And you can stop yourself from doing something you shouldn't do, like throwing a toy.

As we go through the workbook, you will learn more and more skills to help you. And that will mean fewer explosions and much more fun in your life!

Chapter 2

What Do the Angries Feel Like?

Recess Blues

Nicholas is at recess. His best friend, Ali, promised to play tag, but Nicholas sees her playing jump rope. Nicholas continues to play as he looks over at Ali. But he wonders why she is not playing with him.

Nicholas feels his cheeks becoming warm, and he suddenly feels hot all over his body. He begins to remember all the times Ali made him angry. His tummy feels like he ate a brick. He tightens his hands into fists, and he can feel his arms shaking. He wants to punch something but knows he will get in trouble.

Nicholas sees a basketball near him. Without thinking, he kicks it in Ali's direction. He just wants to get her attention. But instead of zipping past her, the ball hits Ali in the knee. She falls to the ground.

Nicholas runs off and hides behind a tree. Ali is crying now, and a teacher helps her get up. Nicholas feels that his cheeks are wet, and he buries his face in the grass. He didn't mean to hurt anyone. But sometimes he feels like he has no control over his anger. His parents often tell him he has "anger problems." They ask him, "Why can't you just control it?" But how do you control something that feels out of control?

In this story, Nicholas was feeling lonely and sad because his friend was not playing with him. He was really disappointed. Sometimes unhappy feelings can come out in ways that are harmful and not helpful—like getting angry and hurting someone.

In this chapter, you will learn the different ways that your body tells you that you are becoming angry. Like an anger detective, you are going to learn to notice when anger is beginning to build up. Once you can do that, you can make a helpful choice about what you want to do with your anger.

Feelings Simon Says

Do you know the game Simon Says? One person plays Simon and tells everyone else what to do. (But Simon can only say things that are safe!) For example, Simon might say, "Simon says stand on one foot." Then everyone is supposed to stand on one foot. But Simon must always say "Simon says" first. If Simon doesn't say that, no one has to do what Simon says.

The goal is to trick everyone by *not* saying "Simon says." It's important to pay attention! If someone does the task when Simon *doesn't* say "Simon says," then they are out. The last person left gets to be Simon next.

Try playing Simon Says, first without any feelings, and then with feelings. The best way to begin to notice our feelings is by practicing them!

Here are different things you can say as Simon. Practice the ideas on this page, and then make up some of your own.

Simon says . . .

Touch your nose	Act like an angry kitten
Turn around in a circle	Act like an angry puppy
Laugh out loud	Pretend to be sad
Pretend you are a basketball star	Pretend to be angry
Close your eyes	Act silly
Act like a kitten	Act grumpy
Act like a puppy	Touch something red
Jump up and down	

How was that? How did you feel when you were pretending to be silly?

How did you feel when you were pretending to be angry?

Becoming Friends with Your Monsters

In the first chapter, we talked about the anger monster. The word "monster" can sound scary. Many people think of a monster as something horrible and evil. But we can also think of a monster as something that is really big and powerful.

We all have an anger monster inside of us, but we also have a happy monster, a silly monster, and lots of other monsters. These monsters are the big and powerful feelings inside of us.

Remember how you drew your anger monster? Now you are going to draw pictures of the other monsters inside of you. You are going to create a monster party!

Draw at least three new monsters. If you didn't draw your anger monster before, go ahead and draw it now. Here are some ideas for the other monsters:

Silly monster

Sad monster

Happy monster

Jealous monster

Love monster

Once you have drawn your monsters, draw in the things that you see at a party. Add hats, confetti, cookies, balloons, cake—anything you would want at *your* party! Show your monsters playing together and getting along.

This picture is your feelings monster team!

It's important that we get to know all the powerful feelings inside of us. When we ignore them, they can start to take over—like the anger monster. When that happens, it gets harder to control them.

When you feel a big feeling inside, imagine your monster team working together to help you feel more in control. This will help you understand your feelings better.

Acting Angry

A good way to know how anger feels is to *pretend* to be angry! That might sound silly, but it's a great way to learn what is happening inside of us.

For this activity, pretend to be angry for one minute. Ask a grown-up to set a timer for you. Once it is set, think about icky thoughts. You can use one of the ideas below or one of your own. If you want, tell the stories or icky thoughts that make you angry out loud!

I CAN'T believe someone took my toy! That's SO unfair!

My parents NEVER let me play video games!

My little brother is SO annoying!

Brushing my teeth is SO boring!

I NEVER get to go first!

NOTHING is EVER fair!

NO ONE listens to ME!

How does your body feel? Where do you feel anger? Are you tired?

Anger often makes us feel powerful. But afterward, we often feel sleepy or tired.

How Your Anger Lets You Know It's There

There are many ways that anger lets us know it's there and needs our attention. In the first chapter, we talked about the different thoughts we have. Many of those thoughts are not helpful.

One way that we know that the anger monster is getting more control is when we start thinking a lot of icky or negative thoughts. Or we start having extreme thoughts. For example, we might think, *Why even try, there's no point?* or *I will never be able to control my anger.*

Let's think about how our body tells us we are angry. Remember the story about Nicholas and his friend Ali? In the story, Nicholas felt different reactions in his body. Nicholas felt hot in his cheeks, and tears came out of his eyes. His tummy did not feel good. His hands became tight fists, and his arms were shaking.

The list below describes different reactions kids have when anger comes. For this activity, start by standing up. Each time you hear a reaction that has happened to you, act it out or point to where you feel it in your body. For example, you could squeeze your hands very tight or point to your tummy.

Hotness in your face or another part of your body

Tightness in your hands, arms, legs, face, or another part of your body

An icky feeling in your tummy

Feeling like your hands, feet, or legs need to hit or kick

Heart beating very fast

Sweating

Crying

Shaking in your hands, arms, legs, or another part of your body

A weight in your heart or stomach

Wanting to throw up

Needing to use the restroom

A headache

Great job! It's important to know how your body feels when anger comes. Your body might even know when you are angry before you do! So, if you can notice your body acting in an angry way, then you can try to do something before the anger monster takes over.

Remember the anger meter? When you start to notice you are at 1 or 2 on the meter, that is a good time to do something to calm your body. Lots of the activities in this book can help you with this.

The Anger Mask

We all have many different feelings every day. Right now, you have a feeling in your body. The feeling could be calm, interested, or even angry.

Anger is a special feeling because it is often like a mask or a costume. When we wear a mask, we are covering up our face. When we wear a costume, we are covering up our body. For Halloween, you might wear a pirate costume or dress up like a princess. Underneath the costume, you are still you, right? Anger is like this because it is often covering up a different feeling or thought.

Let's find out what might be under your anger mask! What's under the mask might change when different hot buttons are pushed. (Remember, a hot button is something that makes us really angry, really fast.)

Here are some feelings that anger might cover up:

Jealous

Sad

Lonely

Tired

Hungry

Nervous

Stressed

Scared

Embarrassed

Hurt

Worried

Fearful

Think about a time when you were angry. What happened? What feelings were under your anger mask?

Taking Care of Ourselves

When we are tired or hungry, it's easier for us to get frustrated or annoyed. This is true for grown-ups and children. But when we take care of ourselves, we feel better. And when we feel better, the anger monster is less likely to take control. This is why it's very important to eat healthy foods, drink water, and get enough sleep.

For this activity, you are going to play a game called Eat, Drink, or Sleep. Here are a few stories. After you hear each story, act out what the person needed. Your choices are Eat, Drink, or Sleep.

Sean was so excited to go to school because it was Valentine's Day. He knew he would get lots and lots of candy. Instead of eating his lunch, he ate a bunch of chocolate. When he got home, his sister bothered him and he threw a ball at her. For punishment, he wasn't allowed to watch his favorite TV show.

Darren was on a bike ride with his family. His mother reminded him to eat something and drink water before they left. Darren thought, *I don't feel hungry or thirsty, so it's okay.* Halfway through the bike ride, he wanted to go home and began to cry. His brother was mad at him because they had to go home early.

Aryanna loved her stuffies. She had 20 of them that she kept in her bed every night. When she couldn't sleep, she stayed up late telling them stories. In the morning, getting up for school was really hard. She usually left the house crying and screaming.

How did you do? Did you figure what the kids in the stories needed so they wouldn't get upset?

Are there times when you don't eat healthy foods, or drink enough water, or sleep enough? Is there something you can do to change that? What are some ideas you have?

Black Hole

What's a black hole, you might ask? Anger is! A black hole is an object in outer space that sucks in everything around it, including light. The anger monster is sort of like that, too. When it takes over, it sucks all the fun out of things that were happening or about to happen.

For example, imagine you are doing a fun activity. Maybe you are reading, playing your favorite game, or making some art. When the anger monster comes out, it takes away all the fun. When the fun stops, you stop what you are doing. But anger doesn't just take our fun away—it makes us really tired.

For this activity, you are going to pretend to be angry. Set a timer for two minutes, or ask a grown-up to set it for you. Have different objects ready that you can use to show your anger. Balls, blocks, paper to rip, and pillows are good objects to have. Think of things that can crash, drop, or be thrown *safely*.

Now pretend to be angry for two whole minutes. (The grown-up reading this book with you can pretend to be angry, too.) Stomp around and jump up and down. Throw your objects and say really loud everything that makes you angry. Keep doing this until the timer goes off. You might feel like laughing (a little is okay), but really try to pretend you are angry.

How was that? You might be feeling kind of tired right now. That's what anger does to us—it makes us tired. It also gobbles up time. And that means we have less time to do something fun.

The Tricky Side to Anger

Anger often makes us feel very powerful. Have you ever felt that way? Sometimes, we say mean things that hurt other people's feelings. Sometimes we even say mean things about ourselves. We also might hurt other people or ourselves or break things. The more anger builds up in our body, the more likely it is to come out in hurtful ways.

When this happens, we might feel super powerful and like we have control. But the way to really have control is to use helpful ways to get our anger out instead of hurtful ways.

Let's do an activity to see how anger can build up and make us feel tired and weak. First, stand up and put your arms straight out, kind of like a zombie or Frankenstein's monster.

Now the grown-up who is reading this book is going to start putting pillows in your arms that you need to hold up. (Blankets or other objects that are easy to stack can also be used.) They will start with one pillow, wait a few seconds, then add another pillow, and keep going.

Each time a pillow is placed on your arms, think of something that makes you angry. Then say the thing really loud. But make sure you don't shout in the grown-up's ear. Try to get to at least five pillows—because anger is big! Hold the pile as long as you can. When you feel they are about to fall, throw them down.

Your arms probably got wiggly or achy after holding the pillows. Do you feel strong and powerful right now or tired and exhausted? Tired, right? This is often how we feel after the anger monster takes over.

If we practice getting anger out in helpful ways, we won't be so exhausted. That will give us more time to do fun things!

This activity is a good one to do when you are already angry. You can say out loud all the things that are making you angry. When you throw down the pillows, imagine you are throwing away the anger.

Chapter 3

How Do I Show My Angries?

Grumpy Goalie

Divya is the goalie on her soccer team. During Saturday's game, she misses three saves. Her team loses by one goal.

Divya is mad at herself because she thinks she let her team down. Then she starts to blame her teammates for letting the other team get close enough to score. Her teammates try to tell her that it's just a game. They tell her that losing is okay and that the most important thing is to have fun.

Soon, Divya has worked herself up into a frenzy. She starts throwing things. She kicks the grass. She yells at her teammates. They give up trying to talk to her, and she refuses to go out for pizza with them.

Divya also refuses to talk with her father as they drive home. Instead, she cries and yells the whole time. When they get home, Divya runs past her sister and brother and goes to her room. She slams the door shut, scaring the cat sleeping on her bed.

In the story, Divya was having a very hard time being okay with losing. She also had a hard time getting her anger out in ways that are not hurtful. The anger monster took over! And what happened? She missed out on fun things, like eating pizza and hanging out with her friends.

Remember, it's totally okay to be angry AND it's okay to get your anger out. But it's not okay to hurt people or things. If we don't learn ways to manage our anger, it will continue to hurt us as we get older.

This chapter is going to help you learn ways to get your anger out after the anger monster has taken over.

Hit-It-Out Target Practice

One of the easiest ways to get anger out is to hit something. There are so many ways to do this!

For this activity, you are going to focus on hitting a target. Get a water noodle or twirl up a towel. Next, take a piece of paper and write down what you are angry about. This sheet of paper is now your target.

Place the paper on the floor. Make sure there is nothing near it so you have plenty of space. Then set a timer for one minute (or ask a grown-up to set it). Now swing the water noodle or towel and hit the target as hard as you can. Hit it as fast as you can. Hit it as many times as you can until the timer goes off.

Practice this activity when you are feeling good. You want to get good at hitting the target. Then use this activity when the anger monster takes over. If you don't have a piece of paper handy, that's okay. Instead, say out loud what you are angry about, and use something else as the target.

If you don't have a towel or a water noodle, you can use a pillow, jacket, or sweater. Just be sure you use something soft that won't break anything.

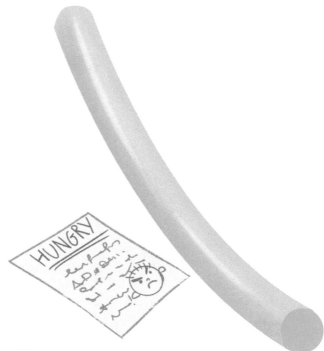

Shame

Have you ever heard the word *shame* before? Shame is a feeling we get when we are very embarrassed or feel very bad about something we have done.

For example, you might feel shame if you threw something and it accidentally hurt someone. Or you might feel shame if you were so angry you broke someone's favorite toy on purpose.

Shame can make us act in ways that are not helpful. Shame begins to build when we keep doing things we are not proud of. It also builds when we don't share our feelings. When we feel really bad about ourselves, there is a bigger chance we will do something we are not proud of—like getting our anger out in ways that hurt ourselves and others.

Often when the anger monster takes over, we feel bad about the things we did or said. This can make it hard to change how we act.

The three steps here are a helpful way to come back from being angry:

1. Say you are sorry to the people you hurt when you were angry.
2. Share why you think you were angry.
3. Share what you could do differently in the future.

Here is a story about a kid who got angry and went through the three steps. It will help you understand how the steps work.

Gotham was at his house, and he was really bored. He knew that his mother had hidden some of his birthday presents in her bedroom. While she was in the shower, he went into her room and found the presents in the closet. As he was looking at them, his mom came into the room and began to yell at him. He became angry so fast he picked up one of the presents and threw it at her.

Gotham goes through the steps:

"Mom, I am sorry that I snuck into your room and looked at my birthday presents and then threw one at you. I felt embarrassed because you caught me doing something wrong and I became angry. In the future, I will try not to be sneaky. And if I get embarrassed, I will try to share my feelings with you instead of throwing something."

Now it's your turn. Think about the last time you were super angry. Then go through the three steps with the grown-up who is helping you with this book. Say your answers out loud.

Twist and Squeeze the Anger

This is a great activity to do when you are really angry.

First, get a towel and twirl it up. Then sit down on the floor. Put both of your feet on the middle of the towel. Grab each end of the towel with your hands. Then pull up with your hands as hard as you can. At the same time, push down with your feet really hard.

As you do this, think of the thing you are angry about. Try to notice where you are feeling the anger in your body. Keep pulling until you feel less angry.

Let's try this right now!

Think of something that happened not too long ago that made you feel mad. Try to notice where the anger is in your body. Once you know where it is, do the towel activity. Keep pulling and pushing until you feel your anger come down.

Story Punch

For this activity, you are going to focus on getting your thoughts and feelings out. Getting them out will help you feel better. It will also teach the anger monster that you can hear it even before it takes control.

You can do this activity with a grown-up. The grown-up should put their hands up in front of you (palms out, facing you, like they are saying stop). Or they can hold a pillow out in front of them.

Now tighten your hands into fists. You are going to punch the hands or the pillow. Punch with one fist at a time. As you do this, tell the story of what is making you angry. For example, you might begin punching and say, "My sister is so mean. I was sitting in the living room drawing a picture. Then she came and ripped it up. It's so unfair."

You might need to punch for a few seconds before you are ready to tell the story. Or you might want to keep punching after you tell the story. If you want, you can ask the grown-up to help you share your story.

Here are some questions for you to think about. Answering them will help you tell your story.

What were you doing before the anger monster came out?

What happened to make the anger monster come out?

What feeling are you having in your body?

Where do you feel it?

What thoughts are you thinking about yourself?

What does your anger monster need for it to feel better right now?

The Blame Game

Have you ever been really mad and thought one person was causing all of your problems? Maybe it was your brother or sister, or your parent or teacher. This can happen a lot of times when the anger monster comes out.

But it's probably not true that one person is causing all of your anger. It's very rare that something is *completely* someone else's fault. The anger monster sometimes gets tricked into believing that it's true. But let's suppose you are angry because of something someone else did. Maybe your friend was mean to you or someone hit you. *You are still responsible for what you do with your anger.*

Here are a few stories. After you listen to each story, talk about what each person did.

Mei was making ice cream sundaes with her brother. He offered her some of the last bit of chocolate sauce, but Mei said she didn't want any. When her brother was eating his sundae, he kept saying how amazing the chocolate sauce tasted and she missed out on having something that was super delicious. Mei didn't like his teasing. She got angry and knocked his sundae to the ground.

Krishna was building a train track and was winding it around the house. His sister Sruti was playing with a Lego set. She asked him if he wanted to make a train station to go with her Lego village. Krishna told her he didn't want to play with her. Later, he saw her village and thought it would be fun to add the train station after all. He added it when she went to eat a snack. He thought it would be a nice surprise. After he added it, he went to the bathroom. When he came back, he found the train track thrown on the other side of the room. His sister told him that because he didn't want to play with her, she didn't want to play with him.

Aaron was upset because his sister refused to play basketball with him. She never did anything he wanted to do. She suggested that they each pick a game and take turns. But Aaron didn't want to play any of her games.

How did that go? Were you to able to figure out what each person did to cause the angry situation? Did one person ever deserve *all* the blame?

Your Secret Power

There are many different activities that can help you get your anger out, at any time. You don't always need to use objects. Can you guess what you could use instead? Your body! That's pretty handy, because your body goes everywhere with you.

This activity will teach you three super-easy ways to use your body to get anger out in a helpful way.

Palm Crush

Put the palms of your hands together, with your fingers in opposite directions (one hand pointed up, and one hand pointed down). Then push your palms together as hard as you can. Push even harder! Most likely your arms will begin to shake. Do this as long as you need to when you are angry. You can even imagine crushing what is making you angry in your hands.

Wall Push

Pretend that you are the Incredible Hulk or another superhero. As you start to get angry, go to a wall and stand next to it with your feet together. Put your hands on the wall. Focus all your anger on the wall and ground. Push your hands into the wall and push your feet into the ground. Push hard! It's okay to move your feet back and forth if that gets your anger out. Keep going as long as you can.

Chair Sit

Stand with your back to a wall. Your feet should be about two small steps from the wall. Rest your back against the wall. Now slowly slide your back down the wall until you feel like you are sitting. Stay in this position as long as you can. As you do it, think about the anger you are feeling in your body.

The "I Just Have To"s

Do you ever feel like you *just have to* do something with your body when you are angry? Do you *just have to* do something hurtful?

Now try to think of some *helpful* things you can do with your body instead.

Here is a list of some hurtful things you might feel like you *just have to* do when you are angry. See how each hurtful action can be changed into a helpful action.

Hurtful	Helpful
Hit my sister	Hit a pillow
Punch the wall	Push against the wall with all of my strength
Rip up my brother's art	Draw something or take a blank piece of paper and rip it up
Scream at my mom	Think of the words in my head or go to my room and say them
Hit myself	Do five push-ups or hit a pillow
Throw something	Make a target and throw safe objects, like stuffed animals, at it

Practice changing hurtful actions into helpful actions with a grown-up. Pretend you are about to do a hurtful action on the list. Right before you do it, change to the helpful action.

Do this with all the hurtful actions on the list. Doing this will help your body learn to do more helpful things when you are angry.

Secret Anger List

When we are angry, it can be very hard to think about the things that will help us calm down. When someone is angry, they sometimes say it feels like their brain is not working properly. You know what? That is sort of true!

When we are super angry, the thinking part of our brain does not work very well. This means that when we are really angry, it's hard to think of something to do to help the anger.

For this activity, make a list of all the actions you might be willing to try when you are angry.

To get you started, here is a list of different actions. Activities from this chapter are included. If you have other ideas, go ahead and add them.

Run around my backyard five times

Do jumping jacks

Throw a ball at a target

Use playdough, clay, a fidget toy, or a stress ball

Go into my room and hit a pillow

Stomp up and down

Jump on a trampoline

Do the towel pull activity (see page 37)

Listen to my favorite music

Rip up paper

Do the story punch activity (see page 38)

Now grab a piece of paper. Make your own secret list that you can look at. Or if you want, a grown-up can show you the list when the anger monster takes control. You can then pick something to do with your anger that will be helpful.

Chapter 4

What the Angries Give Back

TV Tantrum

Miguel couldn't watch his favorite after-school show because it was his four-year-old sister's turn to pick what to watch. He tried to get his parents to let him pick instead. But that didn't work.

Miguel thought to himself that maybe his sister would pick a show he liked. But, nope, she picked something he didn't like—just like always! And not only that, she picked something she KNEW he didn't like. Worst of all, she didn't even pay attention to the show! And then she got distracted and knocked over their milk and cookies.

Now Miguel is really angry. Why does his sister always have to ruin everything? Because of her, his TV time was lost and he didn't have the snack he liked. He decides he's going to do something to get even with his sister.

He finds a drawing that she made earlier that day in her preschool class. He picks it up and rips her drawing into pieces. As he does, he thinks about how unfair everything always is. This will show her! Then his sister comes and sees her drawing all torn up. She begins to cry. She tells Miguel she made the drawing for him as a surprise.

Miguel now feels guilty, embarrassed, and ashamed. He thinks to himself, *I guess I didn't have to ruin her art because I was mad.* His anger then turns to himself. *What's wrong with me?* he thinks. He begins to cry. His father comes into the room and yells that he is very disappointed with Miguel. As punishment, Miguel loses his TV time for the rest of the week.

In this story, Miguel let his anger meter get too high. He decided to get his anger out by ruining an object and hurting his sister's feelings. There are many things Miguel could have done instead. For example, he could have shared how he was feeling. Or he could have done one of the activities we have learned so far.

The activities in this chapter are about what happens to us and the people around us when the anger monster gets too powerful. We will learn more about how to get our anger out in helpful ways.

The Helpful Side of Anger

Yes, you heard the name of the activity right! Anger DOES have a helpful side. Here are a few things anger helps us with:

Anger protects us and the people we care about from danger.

Anger lets us know that something is not right.

Anger helps us realize we feel something is unfair.

Anger lets us know we are not okay with how someone is treating us.

Anger lets other people know that we are upset.

Can you share two times when anger has helped you?

Sometimes we think that if anger gets us what we want, then it's helpful. Imagine a little girl in a store screaming for candy, and her mother buys it for her. It might seem like screaming helped the girl get what she wanted. Right then, it did help her get the candy. But this taught her that she can scream and get angry to get what she wants. That is not a good lesson, and it's not helpful.

Let's go back to the story about Miguel getting angry at his sister. Where in the story did he have a chance to do something else with his anger? For example, could he have shared his feelings, thought about something different, or done something else to get his anger out?

Here are some ideas of things Miguel could have done:

He could have shared with his parents that he felt it was unfair and that he was having a hard time getting his anger out.

He could have remembered that the next time it would be his turn to pick a show.

He could have thought that what his sister liked was just as important as what he liked.

He could have used one of the body exercises to get his anger out.

He could have done target practice.

He could have done the towel twist.

He could have looked at his secret anger list to get ideas.

He could have thought about how he would feel if his sister got angry at him just for picking his favorite show to watch.

Do you have any other ideas of things Miguel could have done when he got angry?

Trust

Trust is really important. Trust means people believe we are going to do what we say. The more we do what we say, the more people will trust us.

But anger can create problems for us. If we can't control the anger monster, we might not do what we say. Or, we might do something we shouldn't do. That could lead to someone not trusting us. How would you feel if your parents or your friends or your teacher didn't trust you? You probably wouldn't feel too good.

Here are a few short stories. Read the stories and think about what happened for the trust to be lost. What could the kid in each story do differently in the future? Remember, we can't change what we did in the past. We can only change how we will act in the future.

Toji's school gives champion awards to kids who do good deeds. At the end of the week, all the winners get their name put into a raffle and someone wins a prize. Toji gets in trouble a lot and feels like he never wins. He thinks his teacher hates him, and he feels angry because he never gets an award. During lunch one day, he saw his teacher leave the room to heat up her lunch. He snuck into the room and took a stack of champion awards. He filled them out with his name and put them into the raffle container. He thought to himself, *That will show her*. Later, Toji won several times in a row. Toji's teacher asked him to come in during lunch time a few weeks later. She shared with Toji how disappointed she was in him.

Cole John was class leader for the week. This meant he got to do special tasks, like taking things to other classrooms. One day, Cole John made cookies with his class. After Cole John ate several cookies, his teacher asked him not to eat any more so they could share the cookies with other people in the school. His teacher asked him to take a plate of cookies to the principal. Cole John took them, but on the way, he decided to eat one. Then he ate a second cookie—and a third cookie. He ended up eating all of them! He came back to his classroom with chocolate on his face. He felt bad, but instead of telling the truth, he told the teacher that he delivered them. He wasn't picked to be class leader again.

Deven was at home playing with his younger sister, Savannah. His mother asked him to play gently and with safe hands while she went to take a shower. Deven said he would, and he and Savannah kept on playing. Savannah kept grabbing whatever Deven was playing with without asking. At first, he was okay with it. He thought about what his mom said. But then Savannah knocked down his Legos on purpose and laughed. Deven was so angry he took her stuffed animal and tore off one of the arms. His sister began to cry. Just then his mother came back. She shared how disappointed she was about what he did.

You don't have to be perfect. No one is perfect! Sometimes we will try to do our best, but still someone might lose trust in us. And that's okay. We just don't want this to happen too often. We want other people to trust us. That's why it's important to get control of the anger monster.

The Hurtful Side of Anger

Sometimes the anger monster takes over. When we are not able to control the monster, anger stops being helpful and starts being hurtful. You may have already had to deal with the hurtful sides of anger.

For this activity, toss a ball back and forth with a grown-up as they share some of the ways anger can be hurtful.

Here are some examples:

Hurting yourself, someone else, or something accidentally

Losing something you like (your iPad is taken away, no favorite TV shows)

Missing out on fun because you are in trouble

Feeling bad about yourself for your behavior

Not getting invited to as many playdates

Not getting invited to as many birthday parties

Losing the trust of other people

Not getting what you want

Which of these examples have happened to you? For each one, share a story about when it happened. Be sure to say what you could do differently next time to take control from the anger monster.

Worth It?

When we use our anger in a hurtful way, we might feel powerful and in control for a short time. But getting angry has consequences—and we probably won't like those consequences. So we need to ask ourselves a question: *Was getting angry worth it?*

For example, imagine that your sister hides your toy cars because she is mad at you. You REALLY want to break one of her toys to get back at her. But your parents have warned you not to do that. You think about how good it would feel to break her toy. But then you think about the consequences. Would breaking her toy be worth it?

When we let our anger out in hurtful ways, it can feel REALLY good at first. It feels like we have power and control. But often this feeling only lasts a few minutes.

Here are some stories. For each one, think about if the consequence of getting angry was worth it. What would you have done differently to avoid the consequence?

Zara was in the kitchen making slime with her mother. She wanted to make purple slime. She put in the drops of dye and began to jump up and down with excitement as the slime turned a lovely purple color. Her older brother came in and quickly put red dye into the slime. He started laughing. Zara screamed, "You ruined it!" She kicked him in the knee, knocking him down. Her mother threw away her slime and sent her to her room.

Walt went to a movie with his brother and his father. His father let him get a slushie and a big box of candy. Walt was really excited! He ate half the candy and decided to save the rest for later. He put the candy box on the floor and continued to watch the movie. Later, he decided he wanted more candy. He reached down for the box and found the box was empty. His father whispered that he didn't think Walt had wanted any more candy, so he ate it. Walt was so angry he ran out of the theater and hid under a bench. He knew this would make his father worry about him and feel bad. But Walt felt his father deserved to feel that way. It took 30 minutes for Walt's father to find him. His father was angry and said that Walt would not get to go to a movie for the rest of the year.

Nikki was at Disneyland with her family. Disneyland was her favorite place in the whole world! Her mother had promised to buy her a princess dress, and Nikki was very excited. When they went to buy the dress, her mother told her it was too expensive. She said Nikki would have to pick something else. Nikki was so angry, she started crying. Then she screamed at her mother, saying lots of mean things. Her mother said now Nikki wouldn't get anything.

How did you do? Were you able to see what each kid could have done differently?

Let Anger Be Your Guide

Our anger can help us understand that we need to say or do something to feel better.

For example, say someone hurt our feelings and we feel our anger grow. Our anger is telling us that we need to share how we are feeling or do an activity to get the anger out. If we do this before the anger monster takes over, we will feel better. This is how our anger can be helpful.

Here are two lists. One is a list of anger hot buttons. The other is a list of things a person could do when a hot button is pushed.

Match each anger hot button with what the person could do that would be helpful and not hurtful.

Hot Buttons	Actions
A. Someone you are playing with says something mean to you	1. Remember that you made the choice to sneak it, so in the future make a different choice
B. You want something that someone else has	2. Remember that you make mistakes, too, then apologize and try to create a plan to remember your jacket in the future
C. Your parents said they would do something and then changed their minds	3. Remind yourself that you have lots of toys already
D. You get in trouble for sneaking screen time	4. Share that you do not like it and are going to play somewhere else
E. You lose your jacket and get in trouble	5. Remind yourself that people make mistakes and say to your parents, "I am really disappointed"

Answer Key

A-4 B-3 C-5 D-1 E-2

You Are Awesome!

It's true—you really ARE awesome! Maybe you have done things with your anger you are not proud of. Maybe the anger monster takes over every day, many times a day. It doesn't matter. It does not change the fact that you are absolutely awesome!

But sometimes we feel the opposite of awesome, especially if we get our anger out in a hurtful way.

In tough moments, it's important to remember all the amazing things about yourself. Remembering those things will help you feel better.

Below is a list of some amazing things about people. Each time you hear something that is true about you, give the person reading this to you a high five. You can also draw a circle around that thing.

Don't worry about what other people say. Only *you* need to believe they are true!

Smart	Kind	Helpful
Funny	Loving	Honest
Good at drawing	Good big brother or sister	Strong
Good at sports		Curious
Good listener	Creative	Hardworking
Caring	Patient	

- -

- -

- -

- -

How was that? Are there awesome things about you that were not on the list? If so, add them to the list.

Jedi Mind Control

Do you want to know a secret? When you control your anger and you get it out in a helpful way, not a hurtful way, you can control the grown-ups in your life. It's true! Well, maybe you can't control the grown-up reading this to you . . . ☺

Think about what happens when the anger monster takes over. Often there is some sort of consequence from your parents. Or you might just feel bad about yourself. That's NO FUN at all.

But when you control your feelings, grown-ups start to trust you more. Eventually, they will give you more responsibility. This will help you when you are older and you want to stay home alone or even get a cell phone.

For this activity, you are going to make a puppet show! Listen to the following stories. Then finish each story in a way that will help the grown-up trust the kid more. For puppets, you can use toys you have, paper bags, or just your hands.

First, here is a story that could end two different ways:

Shannon spilled her chocolate milk in the living room. Her parents had warned her not to take her milk in there because she might spill it. Shannon could feel herself getting angry because she made a mistake. She could choose to cover up the spill with the rug or go and tell her parents, even though there might be a consequence.

Now it's your turn:

Cameron was in her room for a time-out because she got mad and threw a ball at the window, breaking it. She was still so angry she was thinking about taking another ball and throwing it through another window . . .

Finish the story. What could Cameron do that would make her parents trust her?

Here is one more story to try:

Jaiden was in the car with his family. They were driving to visit his relatives during the holidays. Jaiden's iPad was not working and his little sister kept singing a song from the movie *Frozen* that he hated. He could feel anger build up in his chest and then into his hands. He wanted to pinch his sister to make her stop singing . . .

Finish the story. What could Jaiden do that would be helpful and not hurtful to get his anger out?

Your Anger Plan

We have talked a lot about anger so far. And you have done a fantastic job! Now let's bring together everything you have learned so far.

You have learned what your three hot buttons are. You have also learned some ways to get anger out when the anger monster takes over.

The best way to deal with anger is to make a plan. Ask your parents to help you. Make a plan by answering these questions:

1. What consequences have you received when your hot buttons were pushed?
2. For each hot button, what happens when your anger meter goes to 3, or even higher?
3. For each hot button, what could you do differently when the hot button is pushed?

Let's look at an example.

Bindu and her brother Paul often fight about whose turn it is to watch their favorite YouTube show. Her brother sometimes lies and says she is not giving him a turn even when she is. In the past, Bindu didn't give her brother a turn one time, so now her parents do not always trust that she is telling the truth. Sometimes Bindu pinches Paul when he lies and then SHE is the one who gets in trouble. Usually, she is not allowed to watch her favorite show. Bindu feels it is all very unfair.

What were Bindu's hot buttons? Here are some things you might have found:

1. She was not allowed to watch her favorite show. That means less fun. And her parents might trust her less.
2. Her anger moved to 3 on the anger meter when her brother lied. Then the anger monster was in control and she chose to pinch her brother.
3. Instead of pinching, she could do one of the activities we learned, like the palm crush. Then she wouldn't get in trouble for pinching and her parents would begin to trust her more.

Chapter 5

Taming the Angries

Board Game Rage

Noah is playing a board game with his best friend, James. And he's winning! But his mom comes into the room and says it's time for James to go home. It's way earlier than usual.

Noah is about to say they are almost finished, but his mom sweeps all the pieces off the board and into the box. Noah makes fists with his hands. He feels his anger building up.

But as this happens, Noah starts to take deep breaths. After taking five deep breaths, he feels himself calming down. His fists loosen up, and his heart stops beating so fast.

In the middle of the story, Noah was not calm. He was really angry with his mom! But after he took some deep breaths, he was able to get his body to begin to calm down.

Our body has something called a nervous system. It helps us know when we are calm and when we are stressed. Usually our nervous system is calm. But when big feelings happen, like anger, our nervous system gets stressed.

When the stressed nervous system is in control, we sometimes say or do things we are not proud of. The awesome thing is that we have control over it! When we do a calm or happy activity, or think calm or happy thoughts, we can switch back to our calm nervous system!

Remember earlier, when you pretended to have different feelings and tried to notice how anger feels in your body? Just by pretending, you can actually notice how a feeling feels in your body. AND if you practice being calm or happy, you will actually become calm or happy. This may sound silly but it's true!

Do you want to feel more calm and happy? One of the first steps is to teach your body how to feel this way. In this chapter, we will do different exercises to help you with this.

Breathing

You are probably thinking, *Breathing? Really? I breathe all the time! And that has never helped my anger!*

It is true—you do breathe all the time! Breathing is something our bodies do automatically. We don't even need to think about it. But did you know not every breath is the same? Don't believe it? Well, let's practice!

Fast Breathing

Set a timer for 20 seconds, or ask a grown-up to set one for you. When the timer starts, breathe in and out as fast as you can. Keep going until the timer rings. Your breathing might sound a lot like a dog panting really fast.

How was that? The 20 seconds probably felt like a really long time! How does your body feel now? Do you feel calm and relaxed? Or is your heart beating super fast? And is your belly a little tired?

Slow Breathing

Now try breathing in and out slowly. There are a few ways to do this.

You can take a deep breath in as you count one-two-three-four. Then blow it out as you count one-two-three-four.

You can also hold your hands together and when you breathe out, move them apart like a balloon is blowing up. When the balloon is full, take a long, deep breath in as you bring your hands together to make the balloon flat again.

Make sure to do at least five in-and-out breaths in a row.

How was that? Your heart is probably beating nice and slow now. Different parts of your body (like your stomach, arms, and legs) might be feeling pretty relaxed.

Try doing this activity when you feel anger start to build in your body. Take five deep breaths before you decide what you want to do with your anger.

Imaginary Special Place

We talked before about how if we think positive thoughts, we will start to feel better. When we use our imagination to think about something fun, like a birthday party or a trip to Disneyland, we can start to feel better.

Another way we can feel better is to create a special place in our mind full of happy thoughts and memories. When we think about this place, we feel better.

For this activity, think about five happy memories or five things you absolutely love. Then take a piece of paper and draw a picture that brings together all five memories or things in one place.

Here are five examples of happy memories or things:

1. A birthday party
2. A trip to the beach
3. Playing games with a friend
4. A pet cat
5. A favorite superhero

The drawing for these might look like this:

When you are done, look at the picture, or close your eyes to see it in your head. Notice what your five senses are doing. (Remember, the five senses are seeing, hearing, feeling, tasting, and smelling.) You might see balloons and presents, hear ocean waves, or feel the cat's soft fur.

Imagination Superpower

Our imagination is like a superpower. WE control our imagination, and WE can imagine whatever we want! We can create something that has never existed before. When we use our imagination, we can even think things that are not real. And because they are not real, they can't hurt anyone.

This is why our imagination is perfect for helping us with anger.

First, we can imagine what is stressing us out or causing the anger monster to take over. Then we can use our imagination to destroy that thing or put it somewhere else. In this way, our imagination helps us manage the anger monster.

Here are three activities you can do that use your imagination to help you with your anger.

Hand Crush

Imagine the person or thing that is making you upset. Then put your hands together with your palms touching, like you're clapping them together. Push your hands against each other really hard and imagine squishing what is upsetting you. Do this until you feel less angry or you get tired.

Drawing and Ripping

Draw a picture of the person or thing that is making you angry. Then rip up the picture into small pieces. Go to a garbage can and drop the pieces into the can, a few at a time. Imagine that each piece you throw away is like a small piece of your anger going away.

Playdough Destruction

Create a playdough figure for the person or thing that is upsetting you. When you are finished—destroy it! Squeeze it with your hands or give it a good smash. Imagine destroying your anger along with the figure.

Spaghetti Dance and Sauce

Moving our bodies in a silly and safe way is a great way to get the angries out. For this activity, there are two parts.

Part 1: Spaghetti Arms and Legs Dance

Make sure there is space around you so that you will not get hurt. Then pretend your arms and legs have turned into spaghetti noodles! Dance around, with your arms and legs loose and wiggly like cooked spaghetti. Then change your arms and legs into uncooked spaghetti, which is straight and hard. Do this for one to three minutes or until you are tired.

Part 2: Sauce It Up!

After you have done the spaghetti dance, drop on the ground. Imagine your spaghetti arms and legs are now covered with tomato sauce. As you lie on the ground, pretend to slowly slurp up the spaghetti and the sauce. Breathe slowly, in and out.

How was that? Did you have fun being spaghetti? Do you feel calmer now?

Distraction

A fast way to deal with our anger is to do something we like or something that distracts us. (*Distract* means something else gets our attention.) We don't want this tool to become our only tool to help us with the anger monster. But as you work on your anger, distracting yourself can help you move away from anger quickly.

There are many ways to distract yourself. Here are three simple ones.

Ball Toss

This activity is just like it sounds. Get a soft ball and toss it back and forth with a grown-up, a sibling, or a friend. Focus on trying to catch the ball each time without dropping it. If that gets too easy, you can try throwing the ball with your other hand, throwing it behind your back, or throwing it between your legs. Be creative!

21 Questions

For this game, one person picks a person, a place, or a thing. For example, they could pick a superhero, a hospital, or a cheetah. Then the other person asks simple yes-or-no questions to try to guess it. Questions could be: *Is it a person? Is it an animal? Have I seen it before?*

I Spy

For this activity, one person chooses something that both of you can see in the place where you are. (For example, if you are in a classroom, it would be anything you could see in the classroom or through the window that won't move out of sight.) Then the person says something about what they see, like *I see something green.* Now the other person tries to guess what the thing is by asking questions. Questions could be *Is it one of the books on the shelf? Is it outside? Is it a tree?*

When you distract yourself when you are angry, it helps your body change from feeling stressed to feeling calm. Later, when you are back to feeling calm, you can think more about what happened to make you angry. Then you can make a plan to do something different in the future so the anger doesn't happen.

Blow Away the Angries

A wonderful way to deal with the angries is to imagine them leaving your body. If you feel like you need to hit someone or something, hit a pillow first. Then when you feel less angry, you can try to blow your anger away. There are a few ways you can do it.

Paper Airplane

Draw a picture of what is bothering you on a piece of paper. Next, fold the paper into a paper airplane. Then open a window (if it's safe to do so) or go outside. Throw the airplane as far as you can. As it flies away, imagine your anger is blowing away with it. Do this several times if you need to. Once you feel better, you can rip up the paper airplane or fly it into the trash or recycling.

Bubble Blow

This activity can be done two ways. For the first way, a grown-up can blow bubbles very fast. Then your job is to quickly pop each bubble. Each time you pop a bubble, imagine you are popping a little part of your anger inside and letting it go. Make sure to let the grown-up know when most of your anger is out.

The second way to do this is for you to blow bubbles yourself. At first, blow bubbles fast as you imagine blowing the anger out of your body. When most of your anger is out, blow more slowly. Imagine the rest of the anger leaving. As you breathe in, imagine you are breathing in a calm feeling.

Dots and Blow Out

Sit down in a comfortable position. Notice where your anger is in your body. Maybe you feel it in your face, heart, stomach, or hands. Then imagine the anger breaking up into tiny little dots. (You can choose a color if you like.) Slowly blow away the dots. Keep doing this until you feel your anger is gone. You can also imagine the dots turning into a calm feeling.

Yoga Challenge

A yoga challenge is a great way to calm our bodies when we are angry. AND it's a great way to have fun! You can do this activity alone or with a grown-up.

Below are a few pictures of some yoga moves. Start with the first one. Move your body to match the picture. Do this a few times to practice. Then try doing the other yoga moves.

When you are ready, challenge yourself or another person to see who can stay in each yoga move the longest. You can even time yourself to see what your best time is.

Moving your body helps it let go of the anger. Doing the yoga challenge will help you with your anger while you have fun!

It's Anger Time!

Are you ready for something REALLY silly? You are going to set a special time to be angry! Instead of a doctor's appointment, you will have an anger appointment. Set a time for every day or once a week. You can just pretend to be angry. Or you can be angry about something that annoyed you during the day or during the week.

Doing this will help you figure out what makes you angry. This will help you stop the anger monster from taking over—unless you tell it to take over. Remember, you want to make it so YOU are in control of the anger monster. You don't want the anger monster to be in control of YOU.

Here are some things you can do during your anger appointment:

- Say out loud what you are mad about
- Stomp around
- Hit a pillow
- Draw a picture of what is making you mad and tear it up
- Build something and then destroy it
- Act out what happened with toys or stuffed animals

Do you have other ideas of things you could do? Check with a grown-up. If they agree, then do that, too!

Chapter 6

Preventing the Angries

Late to School

Miki missed the school bus because her dad had to take a phone call. A little anger at her dad begins to build up in her chest.

Miki hates being late for school because she has to walk to her seat while the whole class looks at her. This makes her feel embarrassed, and her face gets red. The teacher usually says something like "How nice of you to join us!" Then all the kids laugh.

As Miki walks through the hallway to her class, she tries to notice different things from her five senses to help make her body feel calm. (Remember, the five senses are tasting, smelling, seeing, hearing, and touching.) Miki listens to the sounds of kids in their classes. She smells the yummy smell of breakfast snacks. She looks at artwork on the walls.

As Miki walks into her classroom, she gets herself ready by imagining different things. First, she imagines there is a shield around her that doesn't let her hear any mean words. Then she pictures her teacher as a pineapple! When she sits down, she feels much better. Now she doesn't feel angry at all.

Miki remembers some mornings that were very different. One time she was so mad, she ripped down some of the artwork in the halls on her way to class. But those mornings happened before she learned to control her anger.

In this chapter, we are going to learn different skills we can use BEFORE our anger begins to build up. We want to catch the anger monster before it takes over. If we can do that, we have a better chance of keeping our body calm.

Discover What You Really Need

When you begin to share more about how you are feeling, a few things will start to change. One is that your anger will be easier to control. Another is that there will probably be fewer consequences and more fun in your life!

You will also begin to figure out what is feeding your anger monster, the things that make it big and strong.

Here are a few things that might feed the monster:

- Feeling like something is unfair
- Feeling like someone didn't treat us in a good way
- Being tired
- Being hungry
- Feeling sad

When you discover what is feeding your anger, you can decide what you are going to do about it.

For example, say your anger seems to come out in the morning before you eat breakfast. You will want to eat something as soon as you get up, instead of waiting.

Or, say you find it hard to get out of bed every morning. When you do get up, you are really grumpy! The answer might be you need to get more sleep.

One more example: Say something is unfair or someone was mean to you. You will want to talk with the other person about it, or go to a parent for help.

Let the Inside Out

What's the best way to control the angries? We don't let angry feelings build up and get really big! What we want to do is get our feelings out BEFORE they explode. That way we can use our anger in a helpful way, not a hurtful way. And then we will begin to get control of the anger monster.

The best way to do this is to share how we feel about what is happening. There are so many ways we can share our feelings! Sometimes people think sharing feelings means lots of boring talking. Sometimes we do need to talk. But there are other ways we can share our feelings, too!

Here are a few ways you can share your feelings:

- Draw a picture that shows how you are feeling
- Take a video of yourself sharing your feeling
- Use toys to act out a scene about how you are feeling
- Use words to share how you are feeling with a parent or a friend
- Write down on paper how you are feeling so you don't have to say it out loud

It can be hard to share our feelings. Even grown-ups find it hard sometimes! But the more you practice doing it, the easier it will get.

Share Because Others Care

The grown-ups in your life care about you. So do your friends. And they want to know how you are feeling. If something is happening that is hurting your feelings or making you angry, they will want to know about it. Sharing our feelings is how we build strong relationships.

One way to deal with something that does not feel fair or makes us angry is to use an "I" statement.

"I" statements are really easy. Here is what they look like.

I feel _____ when _____.

All we have to do is fill in the blank parts. That's it! Super simple!

Let's look at the story we read earlier about Miki. She was late for school because her father took a phone call. Miki could say to her father:

I feel embarrassed when I get to class late.

Or she could say:

I feel angry when you take a phone call and then I am late for school.

Here's another short story. After you hear it, try to create at least two "I" statements.

Abby was in the living room watching TV. Her brother was playing with his cars and jumping all around. Sometimes he got in front of the TV, blocking Abby's view. It was hard for Abby to watch her show. Abby kept asking her brother to play in one spot, but he kept forgetting. Abby could feel anger begin to build in her body. She had to make a choice. She could throw something at her brother and yell at him. Or she could share how she was feeling.

What are two "I" statements that Abby could say? Remember to use "I feel" and "when."

Using "I" statements can feel weird at first. But they are like everything else: The more you practice, the easier it gets.

Imagining Your Response

Sometimes, we know something is going to happen that usually makes us angry. This is what happened to Miki when she was late for school. She knew her teacher's comments would make her feel embarrassed and the kids would laugh. And she knew this might get her angry.

What's a great way to change how we act? We can imagine how we *are going* to act. This can help us stop anger from building up. The most important thing is, we want to imagine dealing with our anger in a helpful way.

First, here are some tips for how you can imagine people or things that make you upset. Imagine the person or thing:

- Turning into something you find funny—like maybe an alien with three eyes and green hair
- Shrinking down to a super-tiny size
- Turning into a little kitten or puppy

If the thing that upsets you is a situation or something you have to do, then:

- Imagine yourself as your favorite superhero or animal; pretend you have their strength or any special ability they have (like being able to fly)
- Imagine yourself as a giant
- Imagine you have a shield around your body to protect you
- Say some positive things to yourself, like "I am an awesome person," "It's okay if not everyone likes me," "I just have to make it through this and then I will be done," or "I am in control of my actions"

Now think about something that often makes you angry. Then use some of these examples to imagine acting in a different way. How does it feel?

Opposites Attract

One way to feel better is to put a feeling and a picture together. When a hard feeling is coming, create a picture in your head, like an animal or a superhero. Then concentrate on an opposite, more helpful feeling.

Here is an example of a kid using this idea:

Javier was angry because his father wouldn't let him finish watching the soccer game. His father said it was time for him to go to bed. Javier felt anger begin in his belly. He imagined a picture of a tiger and the feeling of being in control. He pretended to be the tiger and told himself, "I'm in control!" Then he turned off the TV and got ready for bed.

Look at the boxes on page 85. Some hard feelings are listed on the left side. The other boxes list examples of helpful pictures and feelings.

For this activity, think of something you can imagine when each of the hard feelings happens. Then pretend to be that thing. For example, say you are afraid and the picture you create is Batman. Imagine putting on your Batman cape and mask. Then imagine you feel brave in the place in your body where you are feeling afraid.

Add your helpful pictures and feelings to the boxes. You can use this page to remind yourself of the pictures you can use when hard feelings come.

Hard Feeling	Helpful Picture	Helpful feeling
Angry	Elephant, Wonder Woman	Calm, strong
Worried, nervous	A tall redwood tree, a Transformer, a monkey	Brave, silly
Afraid	Batman, a lion	Brave, silly
Embarrassed	Giraffe, a sports hero	Proud, happy

Time Travel

Wouldn't it be great if we could travel through time? We could see what the future is like. We could also go back in time and fix our mistakes. Unfortunately, time travel isn't real—not yet, anyway.

Sometimes when we are angry, we do something we shouldn't do. And sometimes we know right away that we made a big mistake. We wish we could fix it right away. When that happens, the best thing to do is to ask for a do-over. If you get one, then you can deal with your anger in a more helpful way.

Here is an example of a kid who got angry and got a do-over:

Roberta was in the kitchen helping her mother cook. She wanted to cut the carrots, but her mother told her it was too dangerous. She asked several times, but her mother didn't change her mind.

Roberta began to get angry. Why didn't her mom trust her? She was old enough to cut up some dumb carrots. She took the beans she was peeling and threw them on the floor. As soon as they hit the floor, she knew she made a mistake. Immediately she felt guilty.

"Mom, can I have a do-over?" Her mother agreed. Roberta used an "I" statement and said, "When you don't trust me to try new things, I feel angry." Roberta's mother agreed to watch her as she cut one carrot. Her mother also agreed that she would find a kid-friendly knife for Roberta to use in the future.

Do you see how Roberta's do-over was a more helpful way to deal with anger? Instead of throwing something, she shared her feelings with her mom. And then she got the chance to do what she wanted—she cut a carrot!

Can you think of a time when you wished you had a do-over? If you got a do-over, what would you have done differently?

The Anger Monster's Friends

Did you know the anger monster has a best friend? Can you guess what it is? It's fear! (Fear is sometimes called being afraid, scared, or worried.) Anger and fear are best friends because they usually come out at the same time.

Here are some times when anger and fear might come out together:

- You feel afraid of a new situation, like going to a new summer camp or starting an after-school activity.

- You are scared about a consequence you are going to get, like no TV time because you kicked someone at school.

- You are worried you won't get something you want.

- You are worried you will disappoint your parents.

Can you think of some other feelings that might be friends with anger? Here are a few:

Embarrassed	Tired	Shy
Sad	Nervous	Hungry

It's really important for us to know how we are feeling. When we know what feelings we are having in our body, we can control the anger monster and his friends better.

Here are a few short stories. Can you guess how the kids in the stories are feeling?

Blake's mother told her that her best friend would not be going to the same summer camp as her. Blake began to cry and threw her snack on the ground.

Jin hid behind his mother and kicked the back of her leg when they walked into his new classroom for the first time.

Dorie ripped up her artwork when another student made fun of it.

How did that go? Were you able to figure out what feelings each kid had?

From Angry to Okay

Sometimes we can't stop thinking about something we did when we were angry. And the more we think about it, the more we feel bad. This is not helpful for us.

It's very important to let go of things you have done that you are not proud of. You have to leave these actions in the past. You have to move forward.

Here are some steps to help you do this:

- Accept what you did (this might be just saying it out loud)
- Apologize for what you did, if you still can
- Let it go (that means stop feeling bad or guilty about it)
- Decide how you will act in a different way in the future
- Remind yourself that you are still awesome and still learning

Is there something you did when you were angry that you still feel bad about? If so, sit down and draw a picture of what happened. When you are finished, go through all the steps. Then rip up the picture. When you rip it up, forgive yourself for what you did. Then don't feel bad about it anymore.

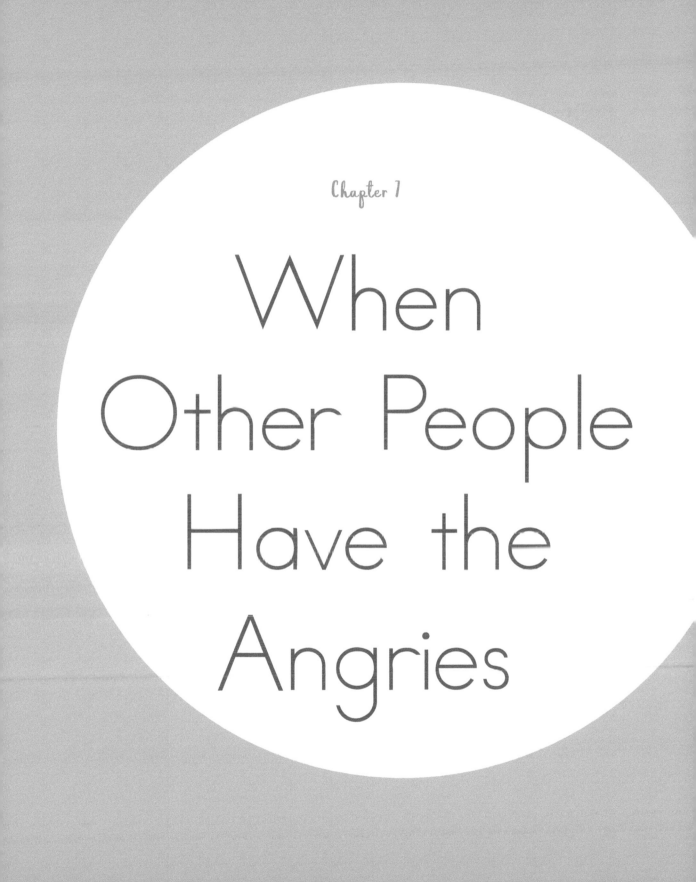

Chapter 7

When Other People Have the Angries

Feeling Better

Mike's friend Olivia made a silly mistake on the spelling test, and she got 95 instead of 100. That broke her perfect record. Mike got 85. It's not his best, but he's okay with it.

Mike notices Olivia getting red in the face, just like he used to. Then he notices her eyes look shiny, like she might start crying. Mike feels tightness in his chest. He remembers how it felt when his feelings used to get so huge he didn't think he could control them. Mike wants to do something to help Olivia feel better. But he isn't sure what to do. He tries to think about what he wanted someone to do when he used to feel that way.

Mike walks over to Olivia and asks her if she is okay. She begins to cry and shares that she is very upset. He asks her if there is anything he can do to help. She says she doesn't know. He tells her that he learned some ways to feel better. Does she want to hear about them? Olivia says yes. Mike begins to share some of the tools he learned, like thinking positive things about himself and taking five deep breaths.

In this chapter, we will learn different ways we can help other people who are struggling with anger or other strong feelings.

Empathy

Do you know what *sympathy* is? Sympathy is when we feel bad for someone. For example, if we see a homeless person on the street, we feel bad for them because they don't have a home to live in.

Empathy is like sympathy, but with something extra. With empathy, we feel bad for someone AND we understand how they feel. We can understand how they feel because we have felt that way before, too. Or it's easy for us to imagine how the person is feeling.

In the story about Mike and Olivia, Mike understood why Olivia was upset about her grade. He felt empathy for Olivia because he used to get upset about things, too.

It's very important to have empathy for other people. It can help us understand why they are doing what they are doing or why they are feeling a certain way. This will help us know how we should act with them.

For example, if your friend's grandmother died, your friend might just sit on the couch and cry and not talk to you. Empathy would let you know that your friend is really sad. You might feel sad, too, because you care about your friend. You would NOT tell your friend about the birthday present your own grandmother sent to you. Why? Because you know this could make your friend feel even more sad.

Try to think about times when you felt empathy for someone else. How was the person feeling? How did you know they were feeling this way? What did they say or do? To show your empathy, what did *you* say or do?

Someone Else's Shoes

Have you ever heard someone say, "Try putting yourself in my shoes"? This is exactly what you just learned about in the last activity, and it is called empathy. Remember, empathy is when we understand *why* someone is feeling a certain way, and we can imagine *how* they are feeling. In a way, we put on their shoes.

When we put on someone else's shoes, we imagine how that person is feeling. This can help us understand them. Then we can know how to talk to them in a helpful way.

Let's practice. Here is a list of things that could happen to someone. For each thing, try to act out what you might say or feel if it happened to you. Think about how you would feel. The grown-up reading this book with you will act out the first one as an example.

What might you say or do if:

Your dog ran away

You lost a game

Someone stole your favorite toy

A plant you were growing died

You missed your favorite TV show

Your favorite sports team lost

You didn't get the present you wanted for your birthday

One of your friends didn't want to be your friend anymore

You got a low grade on a test

You were afraid to jump off the diving board in swim class

How was that for you? Which things were easy to act out? Which things were hard? Why do you think some things were harder than others?

Offering Your Help

At this point, you have a good idea of how to tell when someone is having a hard feeling. You have learned what to do with big feelings. And you have learned what empathy is.

Now let's practice ways we can help someone who is having trouble with their feelings.

Here are a few things to remember:

- Give the person space if they need it (that means leave them alone if they want to be alone).

- Offer your help—don't just do something without asking.

- Remember to put yourself in their shoes.

Here are a few stories about kids having a hard time with feelings. The first two stories suggest some ways you could help. For the last two stories, come up with your own ideas about ways to help the kids.

Ezra was sitting in his class, crying. Another student had stolen the stuffed animal that he brought to school. Ezra was too scared of the teacher to tell what happened.

You could . . . *tell Ezra you see that he is sad and help him find the stuffed animal. You could also help him find the courage to tell a grown-up what happened.*

Ellie was riding her bike with some friends. Suddenly a cat ran across the street and distracted her. Ellie crashed her bike. One of her friends said, "Ellie, you're always so clumsy!"

You could . . . *ask Ellie if she is okay. Ask if there is anything you can do to help her. Share with the friend that what she said wasn't nice. Then say something nice about Ellie to make her feel better about herself.*

Martin was at school and it was lunchtime. His mother had packed his favorite snack, fruit gummies. He was so excited to eat them. But another student grabbed the bag and ate them all herself. Martin yelled at her and knocked her lunchbox over.

You could . . .

- -

- -

- -

Ivy drew a picture of her mother during art class. When she got home, she was excited to show the picture to her mother. Ivy's older brother took out his own picture and said his was better. He laughed at Ivy and stuck out his tongue. Ivy was so mad, she wanted to tear up his drawing.

You could . . .

- -

- -

- -

How did that go? Was it easy or hard to come up with ideas?

Silent Words

Did you know we can share how we are feeling or what we are thinking without using any words? Almost sounds like a superpower, right?

For this activity, you are going play a game with the grown-up reading this book with you. Below is a list of feelings. Each of you takes a turn acting out or pretending one of the feelings—but you can't say any words. You must be silent! The other person has to guess what the feeling is.

Try acting out these feelings:

Silly	Confused	Worried
Angry	Happy	Scared
Sad	Proud	Excited
Jealous	Sneaky	

How did that go? When you practice having these feelings, it helps you know when other people are having them. Then you will know how they are feeling even if they don't say anything!

Helpful, Not Hurtful

We are at the end of this book. Congratulations, anger detective! You have learned a lot about how to deal with your anger and other hard feelings.

You have learned that we are all in charge of our own feelings. Sometimes it feels like someone else is the reason we are angry. But usually this is not true. When we think someone else is causing our feelings, it often means the person is treating us in a way that is not helpful.

It is important for us to understand how our actions can affect other people's feelings. When someone is having a big feeling, there are things we can do to be helpful. There are also ways we can be hurtful. We should always try to do things to help, not hurt.

Here are a few stories about kids having big feelings. For each story, decide if the way someone else acted was helpful or hurtful. If it was hurtful, share ideas you have that might be helpful instead.

Sasha was playing four square with her friends. Every time it was her turn, she missed the ball. Sasha felt so embarrassed. One of the other kids shouted, "Looks like someone forgot to put on their glasses this morning!"

Talia was a new student at the school. At recess, she did not have anyone to play with. She sat down in a corner and started to cry. Bobby came over and said hello. He asked her if she wanted to play with him and his friends.

Jackson was playing tea party with his sister. One of his friends showed up for a playdate. When his friend saw the tea party, he laughed at Jackson and said, "Tea parties are for girls." Jackson's hands turned into fists. He wanted to punch his friend.

How was that? Was it easy to figure out what was hurtful and what was helpful? Did you think of other ways the kids in the stories could be more helpful?

If this was hard to do, don't worry. Just have a grown-up help you practice with more stories.

Resources for Kids

Anything that is hard

Play any game or do something that is not easy. These activities will help you learn to deal with anger. Challenge a friend or a grown-up to a game! But remind yourself, it's just a game. It's fun to win—and it's okay to lose.

Daniel Tiger's Neighborhood

This is a fun TV show about a young tiger named Daniel and his friends. They learn important skills they can use in their life—and you learn about them, too!

Feelings Ball

Have fun with a feelings ball! This ball helps us learn to notice and share our feelings. The more we share our feelings, the healthier and happier we will be! Ask a parent or other grown-up to help you find it online.

Amazon.com/Emotion-Mania-Thumball-4-inch/dp/B0027HGQHA

Inside Out

This is a movie about a young girl dealing with lots of feelings, like anger, fear, and joy. The feelings don't always get along, but they learn to work together. The movie shows why it's important to have all of these feelings inside us.

Mad Dragon

This is a card game that teaches you all about anger—and how you can control it!

NOTE FOR GROWN-UPS: It's important that parents and guardians know what their child is viewing. When parents are able to view, read, and learn along with their child, they will be able to assist their child in better integrating what they are learning. I encourage you to engage in these resources in tandem with your child.

Resources for Grown-Ups

Book Riot

BookRiot.com/2019/04/25/childrens-books-about-emotions

The Book Riot website offers a variety of resources on books. This web page lists many wonderful books to help children with emotions.

Buddha's Brain: The Practical Neuroscience of Happiness, Love, and Wisdom

Rick Hanson

Instead of anger, this book focuses on anxiety, why we have it, and ways to shift it within ourselves. Having a child with difficulties often elicits much anxiety in parents. Therefore, combating this in ourselves is important as we strive to help little ones make their own shifts.

Hand in Hand Parenting

HandInHandParenting.org

This website offers an approach and services to help strengthen the child-parent connection.

Parenting from the Inside Out: How a Deeper Self-Understanding Can Help You Raise Children Who Thrive

Daniel J. Siegel, MD and Mary Hartzell

This is a must-read book for all parents and any adult working with children. It enables you to gain insight into the way you were parented and understand how your upbringing is impacting your own parenting, and guides you in making changes moving forward.

Positive Discipline: The Classic Guide to Helping Children Develop Self-Discipline, Responsibility, Cooperation, and Problem-Solving Skills

Jane Nelsen, EdD

A classic read, this book provides ways to set up natural consequences to assist in shifting unhealthy behaviors. Oftentimes it is easy to set consequences based on parents' own anger or mood, and this book helps parents adjust their approach and shift away from that tendency.

"Teaching Empathy: Evidence-Based Tips for Fostering Empathy in Children"

Gwen Dewar

ParentingScience.com/teaching-empathy-tips.html

This article offers 10 tips that will help parents develop empathy in their children.

The Whole-Brain Child: 12 Revolutionary Strategies to Nurture Your Child's Developing Mind

Daniel J. Siegel, MD and Tina Payne Bryson, PhD

This book discusses 12 strategies that will allow you to connect with your child in ways that help not only your child but also yourself.

References

Campbell, Susan B., Susan Spieker, Margaret Burchinal, Michele D. Poe, NICHD Early Child Care Research Network. "Trajectories of Aggression from Toddlerhood to Age 9 Predict Academic and Social Functioning through Age 12." *Journal of Child Psychology and Psychiatry* 47, no. 8 (August 2006): 791–800. doi.org/10.1111/j.1469-7610.2006.01636.x.

Lorber, Michael F., Tamara Del Vecchio, Amy M. S. Slep, and Seth J. Scholer. "Normative Trends in Physically Aggressive Behavior: Age-Aggression Curves from 6 to 24 Months." *Journal of Pediatrics* 206 (March 2019): 197–203. doi.org/10.1016/j.jpeds.2018.10.025.

Reebye, Pratibha. "Aggression During Early Years—Infancy and Preschool." *Canadian Journal of Child and Adolescent Psychiatry* 14, no. 1 (February 2005): 16–20. ncbi.nlm.nih.gov/pmc/articles/PMC2538723/pdf/0140016.pdf.

Index

Acknowledgments

Thank you to my husband, who supported me in completing this book, along with friends and family. Thank you to Callisto for giving me the opportunity to create this workbook. And most important, thanks to all the kiddos and their parents who have taught me as much about anger as I have taught them.

About the Author

Holly Forman-Patel is a licensed marriage and family therapist and licensed professional clinical counselor. She has been working with children throughout her life in different capacities and settings, including as a preschool teacher and as a therapist in the Berkeley, California school system and, for the last decade, in her therapy private practice. She has also practiced as a therapist for a Head Start preschool program and has worked as the director of a housing program for homeless transition-age youths.

Her specialties include working not only with anger, but also with children and their parents, and with children and adults recovering from trauma. She is versed in eye movement desensitization and reprocessing (EMDR) therapy, a proven way to support individuals who have experienced traumatic events, and assists in facilitation at training sessions in EMDR for other therapists. Additionally, she provides parent coaching to address behavioral challenges and is a consultant for other therapists honing their skills.

She currently lives in the San Francisco Bay Area. When she is not working, she enjoys cooking, gardening, and anything involving comedy.

Printed in the USA
CPSIA information can be obtained
at www.ICGtesting.com
LVHW060410120124
768705LV00003B/25

9 781646 116294